WINGS AND WILDLIFE IN THE WETLANDS

WITHDRAWN

ANNETTE BOELK

1st WORLD
PUBLISHING

WINGS AND WILDLIFE IN THE WETLANDS

Annette Boelk

© Annette Boelk 2009

Published by 1stWorld Publishing
P.O. Box 2211, Fairfield, Iowa 52556
tel: 641-209-5000 • fax: 866-440 5234
web: www.1stworldpublishing.com

First Edition

LCCN: 2009929929

ISBN: 978-1-4218-9100-2

eBook ISBN: 978-1-4218-9101-9

Introduction

In the wetlands the sound of wingbeats breaks the stillness of the day. Though there are many different varieties of birds, they each share their home, the wetlands and environment for their food and shelter and raise their young for survival. Wings and Wildlife in the Wetlands is a book of exceptional photography about birds and wildlife in their habitat. Many of these images were chosen for their unique beauty, reflection, skillful camouflage or simply for the memory of photographing it.

The Horicon National Wildlife Refuge, recognized as a Wetland of International Importance as both globally and state-important bird areas, is also a unit of the Ice Age Scientific Reserve and is the largest freshwater cattail marsh in the United States, measuring over 32,000 acres. It provides habitat for endangered species and migrating Canada geese and ducks, which often number more than 200,000. Nature observation has grown throughout the years and people are fascinated and want to be educated about wildlife. Birds are the attraction to the area.

The Horicon marsh is a shallow peat-filled lakebed gouged out by the Wisconsin Glacier about 12,000 years ago and is located on the west branch of the Rock River in southeastern Wisconsin. The majority of the images used for Wings and Wildlife in the Wetlands have been taken from the Horicon marsh.

Text content was taken from the Annual Marsh Guide/Action Shopper Publication.

Happy Trails and God Bless.

CHAPTER 1

CANADA GEESE

In late winter, when waterways open, the alarming honk of migrating Canada geese can be heard throughout the wetlands. Many have given up migration, making their homes in the wetlands or near open water. The range of these birds is at a steady increase. Pairs mate for life.

Two Canada geese cast their shadow in flight, landing on the icy tundra.

Canada goose taking flight.

Canada goose flight.

Canada geese nest on a hollow bowl of plant material lined with their soft down and can be seen nesting on top of muskrat houses. The Canada goose will also hiss to show displeasure, giving warning to stay away from their young. They feed on grasses, pondweeds, sedges, and waste grains in fields.

Reflections of the Canada geese.

A Canada goose, with its growing goslings, walks along a path in search of fresh greens for food.

Little goslings feeding.

Serenity; A little, very curious gosling walked away from its brood with its parents very close by, keeping a watchful eye.

Two adult Canada geese with a very large brood approach the shore of the wetlands to feed. Males will often act as sentinels, and may become very bold to anyone approaching. Pairs have one brood per year with four to seven eggs. These two geese have a watchful eye over several broods.

Little goslings stay close by their adult parent in the wetlands.

CHAPTER 2

HERONS

The Great Blue Heron, lean and gray, comes from a family of long-legged waders, having a long sharp bill for feeding mainly on fish and aquatic animals. Note its large size, colors and markings.

Great blue herons are the largest North American heron and most widespread. It is often seen stalking fish in the wetlands and will nest in colonies in treetops over water. When surprised, the great blue heron can be heard by its low-pitched barks.

When the great blue heron is in flight it holds its neck in the shape of an S, with its legs straight behind. Blue herons feed mainly on fish, crustaceans, frogs, insects and snakes.

The American bittern is usually found standing alone stalking fish. When in danger, this stocky brown heron will freeze, pointing its bill upward as to camouflage itself with its surroundings.

An American bittern stands along a rocky shoreline waiting for its prey to pass within reach of its bill, and also feeds on a garter snake.

The green or green-backed heron is stalking fish along a waterway, catching minnow after minnow. Green herons are seen alone and inhabit many watery habitats. It feeds on fish, frogs, aquatic insects, and crustaceans. A green heron secures a frog in its bill in the wetlands.

A green heron ruffles its feathers after preening.

The black crowned night heron can be seen perched in trees along waterways or wetland borders during the day. They are most active at night and can be heard with their "quok" calls, taking flight, searching shallow waterways for fish. The night heron is pale and stocky, with short yellow legs, a white face and a black crown.

Heron reflection.

CHAPTER 3
GREAT EGRETS

The great egret is an elegant, tall, all-white bird. The great egret's long, sharp, yellow bill can spear fish in shallow wetlands. Egrets nest in large colonies, and feed on fish, aquatic insects, and frogs.

Great egret's flight, with its black legs trailing behind.

A great egret fishes off of a pier looking over its watery habitat.

The great egret is an elegant, graceful bird in flight.

Great egrets fishing.

These two egrets look as though they are kissing; however, in the reflection you can see the two are several feet apart. This image was captured while walking along a curved path in the wetlands.

Cattle egrets feed in pastures rather than wetlands and are much smaller than the great egret. Immature are all white, and adults have rust plumage interspersed with white.

Egrets nest in large colonies on a platform with one brood per year.

Great egret reflection.

Great egret at sunset.

CHAPTER 4

SANDHILL CRANES

Sandhill cranes are tall gray birds with long necks and red forehead patches, and are among the tallest birds in the world. Cranes fly at great heights and can be seen in a V-formation when in groups. During mating season, sandhill cranes stain themselves with mud, leaving their feathers rust color, interspersed with gray. Cranes probe their bills in the ground for insects and worms, and will also feed on plants and amphibians.

Young cranes are rust color, with very protective parents. Chicks grow very fast for migration in just a few months after hatching.

Cranes have a very distinctive rattling call and are often heard before they are seen.

Cranes perform an elaborate courtship ritual. Birds face one another, bow, and leap gracefully into the air with their wings outstretched, calling to their mate. Sandhill cranes can also be found feeding in surrounding fields of the wetlands.

A white whooping crane with a small group of sandhill cranes was observed feeding in a surrounding field of the wetlands, when the group started a courtship display, a normal activity in the spring when birds are more visible and vocal in choosing a mate. The whooping crane, far right, is leaping about three feet into the air, the sandhill crane at left is about to leap, and the sandhill crane in the middle is bowing. This image was captured in the fall. Sometimes cranes dance for unknown reasons, possibly showing aggression towards one another or possibly when feeling threatened.

CHAPTER 5

WHITE WHOOPING CRANES

Whooping cranes are tall birds, almost entirely white with black wingtips, red forehead patch on their heads, black legs and feet. Chicks are rust color, which helps camouflage them, and they grow up to an inch per day, for their first migration in just a few months after hatching. Cranes nest on vegetation built on moist ground. Usually two eggs are laid, but only one chick will survive for migration to their wintering grounds. The whooping crane is one of the largest North American birds and one of the most seriously endangered. Attempts are being made to breed the whooping crane in captivity. Seeing a whooping crane in the wild is a rare sight. Be sure to respect wildlife in their habitat, remain in your vehicle and observe them from a distance.

These white whooping cranes were photographed at the International Crane Foundation, in the Amoco Whooping Crane Exhibit, within the setting of a Wisconsin wetland in Baraboo, Wisconsin.

White whooping cranes catching a crayfish and dragonfly and thrashing a frog.

White whooping cranes feeding their chicks.

Reflection.

CHAPTER 6

MUTE – TUNDRA(WHISTLING) – TRUMPETER SWANS

Mute swans are identified by their orange-black bill and are more domestic. The tundra (whistling) swan has an all-black bill and nest in the Arctic. Tundra swan migrate by way of the Great Lakes to the Chesapeake Bay, along the east coast.

Tundra (whistling) swan can also be found feeding in the surrounding fields of the wetlands.

Mute swan reflection.

Trumpeter swan reflection at dusk.

The trumpeter swan, the largest native North American swan, closely resembles the tundra swan and is quite challenging to distinguish, especially from a distance. With white plumage and a long neck, the trumpeter swan's black bill is subtly marked with salmon-pink along the mouthline, and is larger in size than the tundra swan's. These birds are submerging feeders; their diet is almost entirely aquatic plants, grasses and grains in fields in winter. These six little cygnets were spotted feeding with their parents in July of 2009, at the Horicon Marsh National Wildlife Refuge, the first to successfully nest in the refuge.

CHAPTER 7

DUCKS

A large variety of ducks can be seen during migration. Some are surface-feeding,while others dive for their food, which includes aquatic plants and insects, wild celery, and pond weeds. The various ducks shown are pied-billed grebe, hen and drake mallard, northern shoveler, blue-winged teal, wood ducks, bufflehead, redhead and lesser scaup.

A drake mallard takes a splashy flight in the wetlands and then shows his beautiful colors during flight.

A female wood duck, identified by the markings of her teardrop eye, parades her large brood in the wetlands at sunrise. Wood ducks have a rather exciting start to life. Hatchlings will fling themselves out of their nest cavity, to the ground or water below. Nest cavities can be up to sixty feet above the ground or water.

CHAPTER 8

AMERICAN WHITE PELICANS

The American white pelican is a very large white bird with black wing tips and a long, wide, orange bill. American white pelicans feed while swimming in groups, herding fish then gulping.

American white pelicans can also be seen in a spectacular aerial display when riding thermals to gain altitude.

CHAPTER 9

DOUBLE-CRESTED CORMORANT

Double-crested cormorants are great swimmers for fishing to find schooling fish, then returning to the surface to devour the fish whole. Cormorants have a yellow-orange hooked bill and are a black water bird. It can also be seen in tall trees with its wings outstretched to dry.

CHAPTER 10

SONGBIRDS

With many familiar songs of birds, when identifying a bird, it is often heard before it is seen. More people are taking to nature observation to feel the frenzy and experience the peaceful harmony of the many species of birds. Songbirds are not only known for their transcendent beauty, but also for the songs they produce. The next several pages are images of a few songbirds chosen for their beauty.

The northern cardinal, a backyard bird, is often seen hanging around feeders with beautiful red plumage. Another bird with brilliant red plumage is the scarlet tanager. His color is to attract a mate, not often seen by bird watchers.

Cedar waxwings are sociable birds, and are found in flocks eating berries and supplement their diet with insects in summer.

The yellow warbler has brilliant yellow plumage. A yellow warbler peers out of its nest along the egret nature trail in the wetlands.

Another warbler species is the yellow-rumped warbler and is found migrating somewhat earlier than its cousins.

The male indigo bunting, with brilliant blue and black wings, forages for insects in the prairies and will also feed in backyard feeders.

The black-capped chickadee secures a caterpillar in its bill along the boardwalk.

The eastern phoebe's call, "fee-bee," derives from its name. An eastern phoebe is seen on branches waiting for insects to pass by.

A song sparrow, here clutched to a cattail, is often heard throughout the wetlands.

The common yellowthroat has a black mask with an outline of white.

The American robin, a common songbird here shown with a caterpillar in its beak, is usually the first to announce the arrival of spring.

In late winter, the rhythmic drumming of the downy woodpecker can be heard. It is the courtship drumming of the male and female. The sun beams through the wings of the male approaching the female. A male shows his acrobatic skills when feeding.

The yellow-headed and red-winged blackbird can usually live near one another with the red-winged preferring shallow water.

A barn swallow displays an unusual view when looking upward. Swallows are often found flying back and forth along the surface of the water feeding on insects.

Hummingbirds have a long, thin bill, combined with an extendable tongue in two parts for feeding on sweet nectar deep within flowers and feeders. The two halves of its bill have an overlap, with the lower half fitting tight inside the upper half. While feeding, their bill is often slightly open, allowing the tongue to move in and out of the interior. Hummingbirds hover in mid-air by rapidly flapping their wings and are the only group of birds that can fly backwards. This male ruby-throated hummingbird was photographed through a window, displaying his tongue.

These female ruby-throated hummingbirds are feeding, backing up and perching on a feeder.

Bees and butterflies.

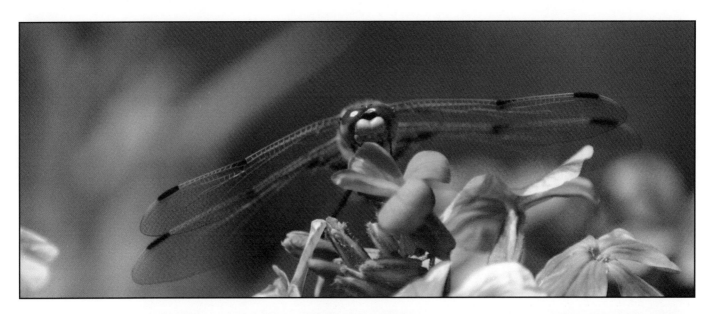

Dragonfly and clear wing moth.

CHAPTER 11

BIRDS OF PREY

The bald eagle is a majestic bird, the national bird of the United States. Adults are dark brown with a white head, white squared tail, and yellow hooked bill. Often seen sitting on a high perch above water looking for fish. Immature are brown mottled with white. Many of these images were captured in Sauk City, Wisconsin, where the bald eagle winters along the Wisconsin River.

Snowy owls can be found further south from their Arctic home due to declines in the population of the lemming, an Arctic rodent, their favorite food. Snowy owls hunt by sight and sound during the day. Snowy owls are powerful and large white birds of prey with gray bars. Females and juveniles are darker than males.

Two little owlets snuggle together in their nest while the adult Great horned owl keeps a watchful eye.

In winter the Saw-whet owl is found roosting in dense conifer trees, with its defense to sit still and not fly leading people to perceive them as "tame."

The short-eared owl has small ear tufts hard to see and will hunt by day by sound.

Osprey can be found nesting in high spots, trees or platforms and are called the "Fish Hawk." Ospreys dive for their prey and hold their catch head first, decreasing the resistance in the air, to make flying easier. In many places people build platforms on poles to attract osprey.

Osprey mating.

An osprey carries nesting material in its talons. Both parents build the nest out of sticks, then line with soft material. The same nesting site may be added to year after year.

The northern harrier can be identified by its white patch at the bottom of its tail. Females are brown, males are pale gray.

Red-tailed hawks have exceptional eyesight. They can be seen anywhere, soaring overhead or perched in trees and power line poles along roads. The red-tailed hawk is the most common in North America.

Marsh hawk.

The American kestrel is found perched on power lines and is the smallest falcon in North America. Kestrels hunt by hovering and move throughout an area until finding prey.

CHAPTER 12

WILDLIFE

WHITETAIL DEER

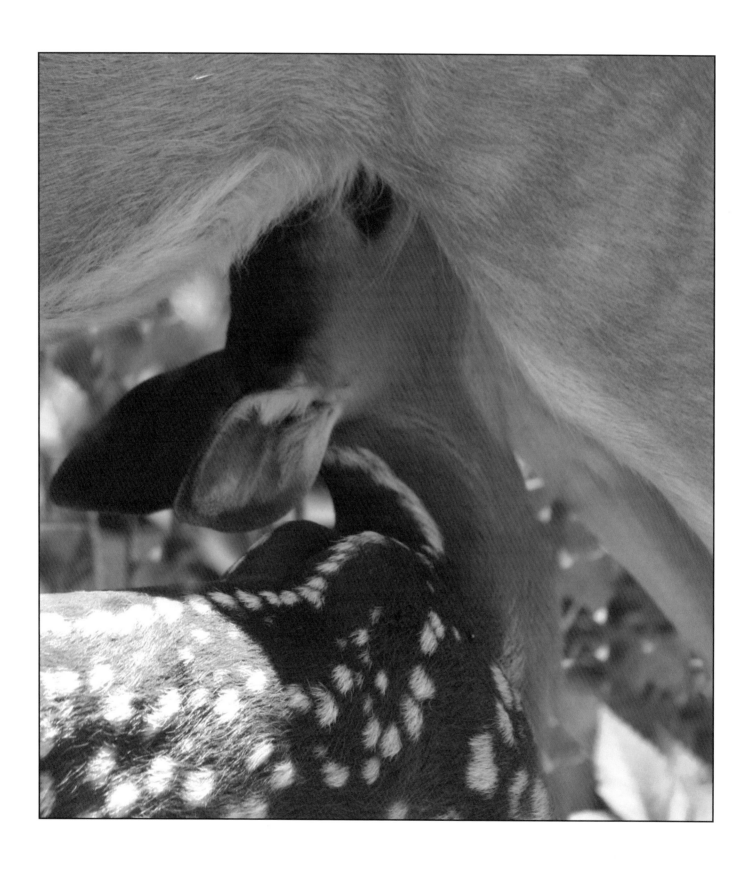

CHAPTER 13

WILDLIFE

A painted turtle is basking in the sun, a chipmunk is found in the woodlands eating an insect and the snapping turtle seldom basks; it is often buried in the mud at the bottom of the wetlands.

Leopard frogs.

A little tree frog crawled into a water can and became stuck in the spout, helpless, looking as though it was happy, with a smile on its face. With help, it was able to release one arm at a time, then both legs to be free again. SMILE and have a great day!

CHAPTER 14

SUNSETS

The most active time to view wings and wildlife in the wetlands is at sunrise and sunsets. Capturing the natural beauty of wings and wildlife in a sunset or a cattail appearing as though it is on fire from the reflection of the sun setting on the water is a unique and beautiful site in nature. Everyone has a story; the amazing part of being in the wild is not just being educated about wildlife in each creature's habitat, it is also about meeting the people there, sharing your story and what you have discovered in the wild with the location. You never know what you are going to experience in the wild. Always be respectful of wildlife and their habitat.

LaVergne, TN USA
12 November 2009
163916LV00004B